This book is dedicated to my younger sister, Lenore Charnigo, who has been to Joshua Tree National Park and loves the Joshua trees.

A Close Up Look at Joshua Tree National Park

By Josie Zayac

Joshua Tree National Park,
located in California.
The desert is awfully hot there.
Don't say I didn't warn you!

Take a close look.
What do you see?
The bark of a Joshua
that's not really a tree.

It's called a yucca
and that's a plant.
Don't ask me to explain,
because I can't!

Take a close look.
What do you see?

Igneous rock-
from volcanic activity.

The light rock is granite.
The dark rock is gneiss (nice).

Formed from volcanoes,
erosion and ice.

Take a close look. What do you see?

The spines of a cactus- so prickly.

Take a close look. What do you see?

Mojave yucca from the desert Mojave.

Take a close look.
What do you see?

A desert
shrub.
Looks dry
to me.

Take a close look.
What do you see?

I see a
jackrabbit
next to
the tree.

Come here,
little rabbit
and play
with me!

Take a close look.
What do you see?

The spikes of an ocotillo.
It's not a tree.

When ocotillo gets water,
it grows 2 inch leaves.
It also grow flowers,
which no one believes!

Take a close look.
What do we have here?

A cholla
(choy-ya)
cactus
with
spines we
all fear.

Cholla cactus garden is found
in the east side of the park.
In the Colorado desert-
but don't go in the dark.

Take a close look.
What do you see?
A paper bag bush.
The bags contain seeds.

Take a close look.
What do you see?

A manzanita- a little apple tree.

Colorado and Mojave-
two deserts in one park.
The Joshua Tree
is its trademark.

Each has its own
type of animals and plants.
What lives in one desert-
in the other it can't.

Facts about Joshua Tree National Park, California

- 1936 Franklin D. Roosevelt proclaimed the area Joshua Tree National Monument
- 1994 Congress renamed it Joshua Tree National Park
- The creosote bush- most common shrub of the park- clones itself. Some are 9,400 years old, making them the Earth's oldest living organisms
- Two deserts make up the park- the Colorado and Mojave deserts
- Joshua trees are found in the cooler Mojave desert
- Joshua trees are yucca plants

Look for other National Park books by Dr. Josie Zayac

- A Close Up Look at Bryce Canyon National Park
- A Close Up Look at Crater Lake National Park
- A Close Up Look at Cuyahoga Valley National Park
- A Close Up Look at Joshua Tree National Park
- A Close Up Look at Redwood National and State Parks
- A Close Up Look at Rocky Mountain National Park
- A Close Up Look at Sequoia National Park
- A Close Up Look at Theodore Roosevelt National Park
- A Close Up Look at Zion National Park

www.ingramcontent.com/pod-product-compliance
Lightning Source LLC
Chambersburg PA
CBHW050930290526
45792CB00002B/952